LIFE, LOVE AND LAUGHTER WITH LIMERICKS!

Nandana Bose

ATHENA PRESS
LONDON

First Published 2004 by
ATHENA PRESS
Queen's House, 2 Holly Road
Twickenham, TW1 4EG
United Kingdom

Printed for Athena Press

LIFE, LOVE AND LAUGHTER
WITH LIMERICKS!

*To Ma for her sense of humour, despite the odds,
to Aunty Christina for her spirit… and to all my
friends who sustain and support me.*

Said a maiden named Flighty,
'I look cute in my nightie,
But beyond compare,
I look best when I'm bare,
And when I'm bare, I'm bitey!'

Said one to the other,
'You seem to resemble my mother.'
After some trepidation,
And much consideration,
They realised that they were brothers!

There once was a man from The Hague,
Who was rather elusive and vague.
He sat perfectly mum
Until he said, 'Hum…
I think I have caught the plague!'

There once was a chap from Quebec,
Who had an extremely long neck.
It was really absurd
To see a small bird
Sitting upon it to peck!

There was a man with a gong,
Who beat it all day, loud and long.
Such was the clamour
Caused by his hammer
That it echoed – on and on!

Standing in front of the mirror,
She cried out in terror
'Cos Gertrude the prude
Caught herself in the nude –
And swore she'd never make that error!

Bambi might be my name
But you'd hardly call me tame,
And though I'm a deer
Nobody comes near –
'Cos horsing around is my game!

What does it matter
If I've grown fatter?
There's a little more of me
That you have to see,
'Cos I'm still the same mad hatter!

Said a lad who'd fallen in line,
'Who will fix this broken heart of mine?
Suggest a cure –
The doctor says, 'Sure,
Fix it with some Fevicol and wine!'

Says a little birdie,
'I ain't choosie,
I like to peck
Just for the heck,
So why don't you be my luvvie?'

A damsel once deduced
That she had been misused,
'Cos when she turned on the heat
He beat a hasty retreat
Which left her a trifle confused!

There once was a guy from Dubai,
Who eyed a nymphet passing by.
Since he was so rude
She labelled him crude –
Which finished the dude from Dubai!

Sighs the man with a pot belly,
'I'm quite undone by my folly,
'Cos when I feel blue
I think of you,
Which only feeds my melancholy!'

Complains a hubby of verbal bashing,
Says he's a victim of her tongue lashing;
'She's such a nag,
That hellish hag,
Don't you think she deserves a good thrashing?'

There once was a guy named Tito,
Who had a bloated ego.
He grew so round
Till he was found
Crushed by his partner's libido!

There was an old man from Peru,
Who differed from me and you,
Because his strange stature,
Was a one-off from Nature –
That inimitable man from Peru!

Said the feminist to the flirt,
'Reform now, or you'll get hurt.'
'How can I possibly fail?'
Cried the affronted male,
And began to unbutton his shirt!

There was a woman who loved to pry,
Being anything but shy.
She called a spade a spade
And wasn't afraid –
Which ensured her success as a spy!

There once was a famous philanderer,
Who fell for a feisty young spinster.
He flirted like mad
Until he was had
And finally became a minister!

Said a guy high on dope,
'How am I going to cope
With such highs and lows?
Yet this I know, and I'm sure she knows,
That she's my ray of hope!'

I never thought it would end like this,
It is your presence that I miss.
What happened to us?
It hurts too much,
So let's get on with the parting kiss!

Said an addict,
'My lungs have quite had it.
Ere I expire,
'Tis my deep desire,
That I should finally have kicked it!'

Out of the blue,
He sat on glue.
Got stuck
In that muck
Without having the faintest clue!

There was a man from Dunblane,
Who closely resembled a crane.
He was buried in snow
Which added to his woe
And compounded his attack of chilblain!

There once was a harridan,
Curved like a meridian.
She misused and confused,
And verbally abused,
Like a character straight out of Sheridan!

A cook, while making rice,
Decided to add some spice.
He waited till the pot
Became nice and hot
Before adding some juicy young mice!

There was a man, strong and tough,
Who was addicted to snuff.
Instead of his nose
He stuffed his toes –
And he knew he'd had enough!

There was an old dame with a daughter,
Who barely fitted in her quarter.
She put her on a boat
And set her afloat
Which solved the problem of her daughter!

There once was a rowdy drunk
Who fell into a deep trunk.
He was hurt
And grew curt
And emerged a trifle shrunk!

A gal once applied some lotion,
And drank a secret potion.
From gladness to sadness
She finally reached madness
Traversing the gamut of emotion!

Bill, the infamous liar,
Got caught in the line of fire,
'Cos he found the opposite gender,
A trifle too easy and tender
And in turn got stuck in a quagmire!

There was a girl who was stout,
Who frequently found she passed out.
She sat on a chair
And nursed her despair,
'Cos she was suffering from gout!

A man most sinister,
Felt he'd been hit by a twister,
'Cos when he stuck out his neck,
He received a peck,
From a most unattractive spinster!

There once was a guy,
Who was so very shy,
During talk at the table
He was quite unable
To come up with a single reply!

A babe, toothy and impish,
With parents bemused and sheepish,
Launched a nuke
And decided to puke,
Confirming his manners nightmarish!

There once was a man from Leeds,
Who sat atop his steed.
Only at night,
Did he alight,
To decorate himself with some beads!

Bridge is the name of my game,
Kings, Queens and Hearts I do tame.
Surely I am the best
Far ahead of the rest,
But what should I do with such fame?

There once was a fearsome wizard,
Who felt a great pain in his gizzard.
Crying aloud,
He opened his mouth,
And belched a breathtaking blizzard!

A sage of yore,
Whom folk did adore,
Got lost in his beard –
Which was indeed weird –
And became a part of folklore!

A promise broken,
A returned token.
Deception, disillusion,
A splendid fusion
For a love long forgotten!

There was a fickle young lady,
Who desired to be steady.
She climbed up a palm
In order to be calm
Which made her precariously heady!

There was a chap, dapper and dandy,
Who fell into a pint of shandy.
He started to rail,
Demanding more ale
And became astonishingly randy!

Jammy's my name,
And cricket's my game.
I'm slow and steady
And it's a trifle heady,
To have fans, fortune and fame!

There once lived a granny,
Who was mighty zany.
She played the flute,
Wearing one boot
Which confirmed her habits uncanny!

There was a young fellow from Turkey,
Who found out that heaven was murky.
He cried out, 'Alack,
It is so black.'
And hurriedly went home to Turkey!

Said a kebab named Reshmi,
'Why don't you eat me?
I'm a nice piece of meat
Who's constantly on heat –
So make sure you never waste me!'

There was an old man with two cars,
Who believed that he was a star,
Such was his psyche,
That he donned his Nike
And took a long walk to Mars!

There once was a man of law,
Who was a mighty big bore.
He landed in jail,
Without getting bail,
And began to nibble and gnaw!

Once a rakish young fellow,
Lured a vision in yellow.
He suddenly thought of Vincent
Who was pretty decent
And became a trifle mellow!

There once was a saucy imp,
Who closely resembled a chimp.
Climbing up a tree,
He fell into the sea,
Where he was swallowed by a shrimp!

There once was a man with a chin,
Which was as sharp as a pin.
It pointed south,
In the direction of his mouth –
What a compass to kith and kin!

There once was a girl from Sweden,
Who left in search of Eden.
But when she was gone
She became forlorn
And yearned to return to Sweden!

There once lived a guy named Todd,
Who was whimsical and odd.
He said, 'If you please,
Spell my name with one *D*…'
As he deemed himself to be God!

There was an old man from Norway,
Who left his wife at the doorway.
He went up north
In search of broth,
And never returned to Norway!

Once a man caringly reared
A long and lustrous beard.
Its colour and size,
Bedazzled his eyes
Which forced him to have it sheared!

There once was a chap from Wales,
Who ate his fish with its scales.
He sat on a stool
And thought he was a fool
And changed his affection to snails!

There once was a man from Columbia,
Who was so very fond of beer.
He finally agreed
To have some tea
And quite forgot the taste of Columbeer!

There once was a sturdy tree,
Who was bothered by some bees.
The buzzing in his ears,
Added to his fears,
Bringing him abruptly to his knees!

There once was a lad,
Who lived only to fag.
Such was his (des)ire,
That he caught on fire
And had to marry a hag!

There once was a man with a nose,
Who wanted so much to repose;
That when he finally awoke,
He found some crows,
Pecking away at his smelly toes!

Index of first lines